DESIRING GREATNESS

DESIRING GREATNESS

KAMARR L.M.W. KING

Desiring Greatness

Copyright © 2023 by KaMarr L.M.W. King. All rights reserved.

No part of this publication may be reproduced, stored in a retrieval system or transmitted in any way by any means, electronic, mechanical, photocopy, recording or otherwise without the prior permission of the author except as provided by USA copyright law.

The opinions expressed by the author are not necessarily those of URLink Print and Media.

1603 Capitol Ave., Suite 310 Cheyenne, Wyoming USA 82001
1-888-980-6523 | admin@urlinkpublishing.com

URLink Print and Media is committed to excellence in the publishing industry.

Book design copyright © 2023 by URLink Print and Media. All rights reserved.

Published in the United States of America

ISBN 978-1-68486-343-3 (Paperback)
ISBN 978-1-68486-347-1 (Digital)

31.03.23

Contents

Introduction 7
Chapter 1: Seeking the kingdom first 9
Chapter 2: Feeding your Spirit 11
Chapter 3: Renewing your mind 13
Chapter 4: Giving Your Body as a Living Sacrifice 15
Chapter 5: Living for God, Jesus, and the Holy Spirit Right Where You are 17
Chapter 6: Faithfulness 19
Chapter 7: Loyalty to God 21
Chapter 8: Answering Your Call and Living in Your Purpose 23
Chapter 9: Obedience to God 25
Chapter 10: Submission to God 27
Chapter 11: Loving God 29

Introduction

True greatness can only come though one's relationship with Elohim, Jesus, and the Holy Spirit.

God inspired me to write this book after I sought answers about life and learned about what it means to be the best you can be.

Sometimes we have a tendency to think as small as an anthill when God's way of thinking is as great and big as a mountain.

And he is more than willing to take you and me by the hand and lead us to the top. And we will not only reach the top but stay on top.

I pray that this book will equip you with the tools you need to achieve greatness.

Chapter 1

Seeking the kingdom first

But, seek (aim at and strive after) first of all His kingdom and righteousness, (His way of doing and being right) and then all these things taken together will be given you besides.

—Matthew 6:33 (AMPC)

Everything we do in life starts with a simple decision. To achieve greatness, one must make the decision to seek the one and only true Godhead: Elohim, Jesus, and the Holy Spirit.

All your answers lie with God, as the word says we must seek God first. This is very important. God is a jealous God, and He must take first place if you are going to ask Him to smile upon your life.

When you wake up in the morning, the first thing you should do is give respect and honor to God by saying, "Thank you for waking me and allowing me to see another day." It is good to read a daily bread as a daily devotion after reading your bible and then pray.

It's very important to ask for forgiveness of your sins and to recommit your life to God, Jesus, and the Holy Spirit each morning before you start your day. If you have time, spend half an hour reading your Bible.

When you do these steps, God moves on your behalf and opens doors. He places people in your life for the days and times you need them and also orders your footsteps. Now your whole day will be orchestrated by God.

Chapter 2

Feeding your Spirit

*And be constantly renewed in the spirit of your
mind [having a fresh mental and spiritual attitude].*

—Ephesians 4:23 (AMPC)

Seeking God and feeding your spirit is an everyday thing. If you look at a newborn baby and compare him to a forty-year-old man who has been bodybuilding for twenty years, there is a big difference in strength.

That's how it is looking at a person's spirit. When a person first comes to God and accepts Jesus as Lord and Savior, God sees their spirit as a newborn baby. But He does not want that person's spirit to stay that way. He desires for our spirits to grow and get as strong as the forty-year-old bodybuilder.

Like a baby, one must drink milk. In the heavenly sense, the milk of the word is nothing more than reading your Bible and getting some surface knowledge, wisdom, and understanding of God's word.

I suggest starting in the New Testament in the book of Matthew and reading all the way through to Revelation. You only need about thirty minutes to an hour a day at first. You can increase your time as you see fit.

Your reading should be backed up by prayer, church, and Bible study. This allows you to get more insight and clarification on scripture.

Chapter 3

Renewing your mind

> Do not be conformed to this world (this age),
> [fashioned after and adapted to its external, superficial customs],
> but be transformed (changed) by the [entire] renewal of your
> mind [by its new ideals and new attitude], so that you may
> prove [for yourselves] what is the good and acceptable and
> perfect [in his sight for you].
>
> —Romans 12:2 (AMPC)

This is very important because your mind controls your actions and behaviors. Before accepting Jesus as Lord, and not having read God's word, we all were carnal minded. This is a worldly way of thinking. The only book or word that is truth that has the power to renew one's mind to right thinking is the Holy Bible. It is God's divine knowledge, wisdom, and understanding. It is the only truth.

Once you believe the word and line your thinking up with God's way of thinking, you will be on the road to greatness. I believe that the word of God should be read daily, along with a spiritual book. Here are a few to start with:

- Joyce Meyer, *Battlefield of the Mind and The Word, the Name, the Blood*
- Rick Warren, *Purpose Driven Life*
- David G. Evans, *Dare to be a Man*
- T.D. Jake's, *Speaks to Men and Reposition Yourself*
- Robert Kiyosaki, *Rich Dad, Poor Dad and Guide to Investing*

Chapter 4

Giving Your Body as a Living Sacrifice

*I appeal to you therefore Brethren and beg of you in view of [all]
the mercies of God, to make a decisive dedication of your
bodies [presenting all your members and
faculties] as a living sacrifice,
Holy [devoted consecrated] and well pleasing to God, which is your
reasonable (rational, intelligent) service and spiritual worship.*

—Romans 12:1

Your body is the temple of the Holy Spirit. You should monitor what you eat and drink and should not allow any foreign chemicals into your body (e.g., cigarettes, alcohol, street drugs). Also, be careful of prescriptions drugs. Do not abuse them.

Exercise is very important. It is necessary to do a cardio workout at least four times a week for thirty minutes at a time. The days when you are not doing cardio, do some weight training. Do not do cardio and weights on the same day. You will put too much stress on your body at one time.

It is very important to flush your bowels once or twice a week. This keeps unwanted waste out of your system and reduces your chances for sickness and disease. You can take an over-the-counter total body cleanser with some water. This is a slow-working laxative. Coffee can help the flushing process. It is a natural laxative as well. The process works best on an empty stomach.

Diet and exercise go hand in hand. It is very important to eat a low-carb diet with a good amount of protein. You will get the best results doing so.

Chapter 5

Living for God, Jesus, and the Holy Spirit Right Where You are

*[After all] the kingdom of God is not a matter of [getting the]
food and drink [one likes] but instead it is
righteousness (that state which make a person acceptable to God)
and [heart] peace and joy in the Holy Spirit. He who serves
Christ in this way is acceptable and pleasing
to God and is approved by men.*

—Romans 14:17-18 (AMPC)

A servant is not more than his master. Because Jesus came to earth to serve man and not to be served, you will have to allow God to you use you right where you are in your life.

Know that there are many ways to be a servant unto God. You can serve in your home church, or you can help the needy and buy some clothes or something to eat.

Personally, I feel one of the best ways to serve is sharing the good news of salvation through Jesus with others. Jesus is the greatest gift of all; you can share it with words or by your walk.

When you start to be used by God and you're walking in servanthood, you will experience the greatest peace and joy you have ever known.

Chapter 6

Faithfulness

Because you have guarded and kept My word of patient endurance [have held fast the lesson of My patience with the expectant endurance that I give you], I also will keep you [safe] from the hour of trails (testing) which is coining on the whole world to try those who dwell upon the earth.

—Revelation 3:10 (AMPC)

Faithfulness is your allegiance to your duty as a Christian. It is also allegiance to God. You prove your love to God, Jesus and Holy Spirit to be genuine through your faithfulness.

Faithfulness is when you have a situation where a tragedy comes in your life. Your countenance may fall a little, but you read your Bible and pray to God and hold on to Him, even still. It is staying true to God no matter what comes your way. When Jesus sees that you are faithful after being tested, He will trust you with your purpose and other people's lives.

Chapter 7

Loyalty to God

Fear nothing that you are about to suffer. [Dismiss your dread and your fears!] Behold, the devil is indeed about to throw some of you into prison, that you may be tested and proved and critically appraised, and for ten days you will have affliction. Be loyally faithful unto death [even if you must die for it], and I will give you the crown of life.

—Revelation 2:10 (AMPC)

Loyalty is a lot like being faithful, but it is for a lifetime. It is basically being consistent, or never turning your back on God no matter what comes your way. *For God I live, and for God I die.* We are soldiers of God's army, fighting a spiritual war against Satan and all his demons. So, know that your life is on the line. Be encourage to be loyal and stand on the ground on God's battlefield. You are fighting the good fight of faith, having the most powerful weapon of all—a two-edged sword, which is the word of God.

Chapter 8

Answering Your Call and Living in Your Purpose

*We are assured and know that [[a]God being a partner in
their labor] all things work together and are [fitting into a plan]
for good to and for those who love God and
are called according to [His] design and purpose.*

—Romans 8:28 (AMPC)

God calls every man and woman to live for Him. The question is. will you say yes to Jesus with a sincere heart? Saying yes to Jesus means living according to God's sayings or His commandments to your absolute best.

It also means that you take on some responsibilities that Jesus has handed down to us. The first is the great commission to tell others about Jesus and how they may gain salvation through Him. You posses other purposes, and only Jesus can tell you what they are. When you begin to live for God and do things He has said to do, then you will know the very reason you were born into this world. Then you will have peace, joy, and fulfillment of life.

Live in your purpose, and watch God open the windows of heaven for you and pour down blessings and favor.

Chapter 9

Obedience to God

*And after He had appeared in human form,
He abased and humbled Himself [still further] and
carried His obedience to the extreme of death,
even the death of the cross!*

—Philippians 2:8 (AMPC)

In serving God, there is no room for stubbornness or not listening. You must learn to be obedient at all times. Jesus wants to know that you trust Him and understand that He has your best entrust at heart.

Please know Elohim, Jesus, and the Holy Spirit are not your enemies. Let them love on you, lead you, and guide you right into greatness. You may experience a bump in the road, so go slow and put your seat belt on. I encourage you to stay in the car with Jesus and endure the ride. The main thing is that you remember that Jesus is the driver. All you do is what you are asked.

Chapter 10

Submission to God

*But He gives us more and more grace (power of the
Holy Spirit, to meet this evil tendency and all others fully).
That is why He says, God sets Himself against the proud and
haughty, but gives grace [continually] to the lowly
(those who are humble enough to receive it).
So be subject to God. Resist the devil [stand firm against him],
and he will flee from you.*

—James 4:6-7 (AMPC)

To submit to God means that you are yielding to Him or being subject to him. Know that He overpowers you. It behooves you to allow God to overpower you and allow Him to control your life. Remember that He only wants what's best for you.

True submission to God, Jesus, and the Holy Spirit means that you let go of all your fleshly desires, like drinking alcohol and smoking. Instead you line your will up with God's will and do all that He asks of you.

Lining your will up with God's will entails reading or studying your Bible and going to church and Bible study. Also, after you have heard from God on what your purpose is, learn all there is to know about your purpose and prepare yourself every day to do your best in your purpose that God has placed on your life.

Chapter 11

Loving God

And you shall Love the Lord your God with all your [mind and] heart and with your entire being and with all your might.

—Deuteronomy 6:5 (AMPC)

I left this one for last because it is most important. Loving God with all your mind, all your soul, all your heart, and all your strength is a choice. There may be times when God may put you through some learning lessons, and not all the time do they feel good or like the worldly way of love. We tend to think that love is a warm, fuzzy feeling that always feels good. But God's way of showing love is not always so. 2 Timothy 3:12 says, "Indeed all who delight in piety and are determined to live a devoted and Godly life in Christ Jesus will meet with persecution [will be made to suffer because of their religious stand]." It also says in 1 Peter 1:6-7,

[You should] be exceedingly glad on this account though now for a little while you may be distressed by trials and suffer temptations so that the [genuineness] of you faith may be tested [your faith] which is infinitely more precious than the perishable gold which is tested and purified by fire. [This proving of your faith is intended] to redound to [your] praise and glory and honor when Jesus Christ [the Messiah, the Anointed One] is revealed.

The word also says that God will chasten and correct those he loves. These things don't always feel like love, but know that God does love you, and we have to choose to love Him knowing that He is God, Creator of heaven and earth, and He formed you in your mother's womb. He has your best interest at heart. The word says that God is a jealous God, and He wants to know that you love Him more than anyone or anything else. When you prove that He is your first true love, then you will see that everything else you have read about will fall right in line, and you will receive God's favor and blessings. I encourage you to fall in love with Elohim, Jesus, and the Holy Spirit, and I promise you will be loved back.

Last Words

By applying these tools, one is actually living a life of worship unto Elohim, Jesus, and the Holy Spirit. And you are worshiping mind, body, and spirit, which gives you harmony.

In doing these very necessary steps, you are partnering up with God, and we know that all things are possible for God. He is the one who gives you the seed to sow and the strength or power to plow and spread the seed, then gives you rain and sun to bring the increase. Then He gives you more strength and power to reap the harvest.

I pray that these lessons have given you some insight in your spiritual life and have better equipped you to be stronger altogether for the glory of God.

Understand that this is a spiritual journey and is a process of climbing the mountain. If you apply all that is in this book, our God and Father, Jesus, and the Holy Spirit will make sure that you reach the top. I encourage you to be strong and courageous and be a servant of our Lord and Master. Let Him live through you. Living for Jesus is a lifestyle! He not only wants you to win, but He will also make you win.

I pray that you yield your will to God's will and that you fall in love with Jesus, allowing him to be the author and finisher of your faith to do all things.

May Elohim, Jesus, and the Holy Spirit
bless you and your household.

Brother: KaMarr L.M.W. King

www.ingramcontent.com/pod-product-compliance
Ingram Content Group UK Ltd.
Pitfield, Milton Keynes, MK11 3LW, UK
UKHW050412240426
12048UKWH00020B/1473